4.11.78

STOP LETTING PEOPLE WALK ALL OVER YOU!

Are you timid? Wishy-washy? Are you the kind of wimp who thanks the policeman after getting a ticket? Have you run out of cheeks to turn?

Chances are you're one of millions of Americans who are manic concessive. People who cave in at the slightest suggestion of stress or conflict. And chances are you've dragged yourself through the trauma of Assertion Training only to discover that your cowardice is a cancer, not a bruise.

You Can *Run Away from It!* is a book about hope. About not being ashamed about "that" anymore. About Julian Meeker's revolutionary Concession Training. About one hundred pages of insight that reveal to you the survival secrets of the Ancients: Avoidance, Suppression, and Rationalization.

Early man said it best when he said, "Oh, shit, a dinosaur! Let's get the hell out of here!" He survived because he learned to recognize his predators and accept his limitations. Concession Training teaches you how to recognize *your* predators. How to smile in the face of adversity. How to whimper with dignity. How to run from threatening persons as you repeat over and over the Concession Training mantra, "Oh, God, please make them leave me alone!"

Remember, loud and aggressive persons are more than vexations to the spirit. They could kill you! This beautiful book could save your life.

YOU CAN RUN AWAY FROM IT!

J. B. Lippincott Company
Philadelphia and New York

Julian Meeker

YOU *CAN* RUN AWAY FROM IT!

Rewritten by R. Tim Philen

CREDITS

Illustrations

R. Tim Philen: 21, 22, 24, 52, 53, 54, 102, 103, 104
Kelly Coy: 82, 83, 84

Photography
James Girard

Unending encouragement and support to the author
Don Girard

Intellect and sympathy
Paul Butler

U.S. Library of Congress Cataloging in Publication Data

Philen, R. Tim.
  You can run away from it!

  1. Assertiveness (Psychology)—Anecdotes, facetiae,
satire, etc.   I.   Meeker, Julian, You can run away from
it!   II.   Title.
BF575.A85P47   158.1'0207   78-1481
ISBN-0-397-01282-9

Contents

Author's Note

First of all, I'd like to apologize for not writing sooner. I've had this book nearly complete for two years now, but frankly I was afraid of losing the few friends that I can trust by appearing to be dealing in "one-upmanship," seeing as none of them has had material published.

Secondly, I must apologize for my rhetorical and grammatical inconsistencies. My English teacher died when I was very young, so I was forced to learn clarity in exposition from my grandfather's lawbooks. Fortunately, I was able to cut down my lengthy original manuscript, replete with run-on sentences, by having the rewrite done by a haiku poet.

Consequently, I am very sorry for the shortness of the book. Doesn't seem like much for the money, I know, but my dear mother has been ill, and my older sister has been hounding me for the back rent. Believe me, I'll make it up to you somehow!

JULIAN MEEKER
Santa Monica, California

1

The Neurotic Need for Concession Training

No arts; no letters; no society;
and which is worst of all, continual
fear and danger of violent death;
and the life of man, solitary, poor,
nasty, brutish and short.

THOMAS HOBBES

THE SACRED BIAS

America is a nation built and sustained by aggressive and ambitious individuals. To survive happily in this society, one must have a tolerance, if not a lust, for stress and competition. From the moment we're born, the idea of "winners and losers" is ingrained into our thinking. Our educational system promotes competition. Our free-enterprise economy demands it. Violence in the media glorifies it. And with it all comes an enormous backlash of bias against the puny, the weak, the cowardly.

Elmer Davis spoke for many Americans when he asserted, "This Republic was not established by cowards, and cowards will not preserve it!"[1] True as that may be, even a casual glance at the Declaration of Independence would have reminded Mr. Davis that cowards have the same inalienable rights as every other American.

Still, the bias is sacred. So sacred that even enlightened psychologists have resisted offering

[1] *But We Were Born Free,* 1936.

a dignified absolution and encouragement to cowards. Odd indeed, since it is the psychological community that has always been at the forefront of myth destruction—always anxious to disprove archaic (and much-cherished) notions about the "deviance" of certain nonconformist behaviors. They've helped set the record straight about the "horrible consequences" of masturbation instilled in us by our parents. They've encouraged homosexuals to come out of the closet and stand up for their right to go against the grain in this heterosexual-dominated society. They've even advised candidates for transsexual operations to listen to the ever-present urgings of their alter gender, no matter the cost.

Yet when they address the "problem" of cowardice in Assertiveness Training, they purposely relate only to those unassertive persons who have at least enough courage and mental stability to assimilate into the assertive mainstream. They benignly neglect the nearly 4 million Americans[2] who are "Manic Conces-

---

[2]Based on statistics cited in *Abnormal Psychology and Modern Life* by James C. Coleman and William E. Broen, Jr., anxiety neurotics comprise 30 to 40 percent of the estimated 10 million neurotic individuals in the United States.

sives"—who have been courage-impaired since birth—who lack even the basic adjustive skills necessary to implement Assertiveness Training precepts into their daily lives.[3]

Simply, Assertiveness Training is for people I would term "Simple Unassertives": people who want power and respect but don't know how to get it; people who want more control over their lives but have trouble saying no; people who want a bigger piece of the pie and can learn to fight for it.

Concession Training is for people who just want to be left alone; people who need time to sort out whatever pieces of psyche they can still find; people who have been programmed to hate themselves because they cannot emulate the norm; people—Manic Concessives—who may have tried Assertiveness Training and were shocked to discover that batteries were not included, that intellectualizing about being assertive and actually *being* assertive are palpitations apart!

Case

Myron M. came to my office after a disastrous experience with Assertiveness Training

[3]See appendix.

techniques. Two months earlier he had picked up a book on AT and was ecstatic about how easy it sounded to speak up and get what you want from people. He was particularly taken by a technique called "Slipped Disc," in which the unassertive person, unswerved by threats and manipulation, repeats his request over and over until the aggressive person gives him what he wants. One case history Myron read had to do with a person who had somehow misplaced his meat leaving a supermarket and had returned to get it. He simply kept repeating his request *"I want my meat!"* ignoring the harassment of the checker and butcher. Thanks to Slipped Disc, he walked out of the store the victor, meat in hand.

A few days later, Myron experienced a similar problem and summoned up the nerve to try Slipped Disc for himself. Following is the verbal exchange as Myron related it:

Myron approaches the checkstand where he had purchased a roasting duck for his dinner.

MYRON *(politely but firmly):* Excuse me, sir!

No response from checker, who is busy ringing up items for a customer.

MYRON *(clearing his throat):* Excuse me! My name is Myron M. I bought a roasting duck here about a half hour ago, and you evidently forgot to put it in the bag. I got home and realized the mistake. Now I'm back, and I want my duck, please!

CHECKER *(turning around):* Yeah, I remember you, but I don't remember any duck laying around after you. Why don't you look in your car or check back home.

MYRON *(eyes closed, breathing harder):* I got home and realized the mistake. Now I'm back, and I want my duck, please! [SLIPPED DISC]

CHECKER *(to next customer in line):* Hi, how are you today? [REJECTION]

MYRON: Uh...excuse me! Now I'm back, and I want my duck! [SLIPPED DISC]

CHECKER *(visibly annoyed, turns to intercom):* Louie to Checkstand Four, Louie to Checkstand Four. *(The head butcher, a 240-pound hulk with a handlebar mustache and "Eat My Pud" embroidered on his apron, approaches the checkstand, visibly disgruntled, as if he resents being interrupted. The checker points to Myron. The butcher motions Myron to follow him. Temporarily relieved, Myron follows to a back room, a-stink with the smell of animal entrails. This begins to nauseate him.)*

LOUIE: What's the trouble, *sir?* [INTIMIDATION]

MYRON *(beginning to feel ill):* My...uh ...name is Myron. I...uh...bought a duck here about a half hour ago, and the checker evidently forgot to put it in the bag. I got home—

LOUIE *(interrupting):* Did he *say* he forgot to put it in the bag?

MYRON: Well...uh...no....

LOUIE: Well then, look back home or in your car.

MYRON *(staring at his shoes):* Well...I... uh...got home and realized the mistake. It wasn't at home and it wasn't in the car.

LOUIE *(glaring):* Well, *sir,* maybe it just flew back into the meat counter, because if *you* don't have it, and the *checker* doesn't have it, then *you* never paid for it! Now you're taking up my time with some GODDAMNED DUCK THAT NEVER LEFT THE STORE AND THAT YOU NEVER PAID FOR! *(Other butchers stop what they're doing and begin to stare at Myron.)*

MYRON *(feeling the onset of an anxiety attack):* Oh, well, I'm...uh...sorry....I...uh...didn't realize you were so busy. I'll...uh...just check back home or...uh...in my car, I guess, whatever...uh...

Myron stumbled out of the supermarket, traumatized, embarrassed, and guilty about having lost the battle. "If only the butcher had been a sweet old lady," he lamented, "I could have maintained presence of mind." So unable to make a scene, so intimidated by the butcher's physical presence and threatening tone, Myron completely forgot that he had the receipt, the proof of purchase, in hand the entire time. After returning home he calmed down enough to realize his mistake. Not wanting to risk the nervous anxiety again, however, he never returned to the market. His self-confidence at an all-time low, he came to my office for help.

THE BEHAVIORIST TRAP

Assertiveness Training therapies share a common behaviorist premise: that unassertive behaviors are learned habits (conditioned responses to stimuli) that can be unlearned by systematically reinforcing (rewarding) new, assertive responses to the stimuli and, at the same time, punishing (not rewarding) the continuation of "wrong" unassertive responses. The net result (as proven by the carefully selected case studies in AT handbooks) is the eradication of *symptoms* of unassertive behavior.

This *"Mechanix Illustrated* for the Mind" approach to assertiveness is certainly a siren song to unassertive persons. But, as we saw in the case of Myron M., it amounts to a continuation of the sacred bias. Manic Concessives are Compound Unassertives, not Simple Unassertives who can be expected to possess enough singleness of purpose and intestinal fortitude to respond assertively to threatening stimuli in real-world situations. For the Manic Concessive, whose cerebral circuitry reads like a *Who's Who* of frayed neuron endings, behaviorist techniques can only lead to more trauma.

Case

Since his teenage years, Robert T. had been extremely girl-shy. Asking for a date over the telephone was still a traumatic experience. Frozen by fear of rejection, he invariably handled the call awkwardly, coming off as a bumbling flake. His self-image deteriorated to the point where he lived in fear and loathing of the telephone's ringing. It was a painful reminder of unrequited love. In desperation, Robert sought out a behavior-modification therapist.

The therapist told him that his conditioned response to the ringing phone was anxiety caused by fear of rejection (unassertive behavior). The desirable response was answering the telephone and communicating directly and openly with the party (assertive behavior).

The therapist asked him to name a favorite pleasure other than sex. Robert said ice cream. The therapist advised Robert to think of ice cream every time the phone rang. If it was a particularly long, insistent ring, he was to think of different flavors of ice cream until the ringing stopped. When Robert got up the courage to actually answer the phone, he was allowed to reward himself with a dish of ice cream.

Thus, Robert began to associate the ringing phone with something pleasurable (ice cream) instead of something traumatic (rejection). Within two months the situation had turned completely around. Robert actually began to look forward to the phone's ringing and even managed to initiate calls to ask girls out on dates.

When he came to my office six months later, however, Robert was once again nervous and girl-shy. It seems that while he did gain confidence through the behavior therapy, he also gained forty pounds. When a date would see the body "that lean, muscular voice was trapped in," she would turn off, shaking Robert's confidence. As the evening regressed from one already-asked question to the next, Robert's insecurity would double and triple, until the only way he could keep from having an anxiety attack was to change the subject to ice cream. He would start talking nonstop about everything from pistachio nut blight to the sociopolitical impact of the Milk Advisory Board. Before long he was dragging his dates to ice cream parlors and dairy tours—novelties that wore out quickly. Robert's new fear of rejection began to permeate his life. His new addiction to ice cream began to drain his insulin supply. He was once again a traumatized, broken man.

THE NEUROTIC PARALLEL

When we speak of the difference between Simple Unassertives and Manic Concessives, we are really speaking of different degrees of a condition known as neurosis. Unlike neuritis and neuralgia, neurosis is a maladjustment in the coping mechanisms one employs in dealing with

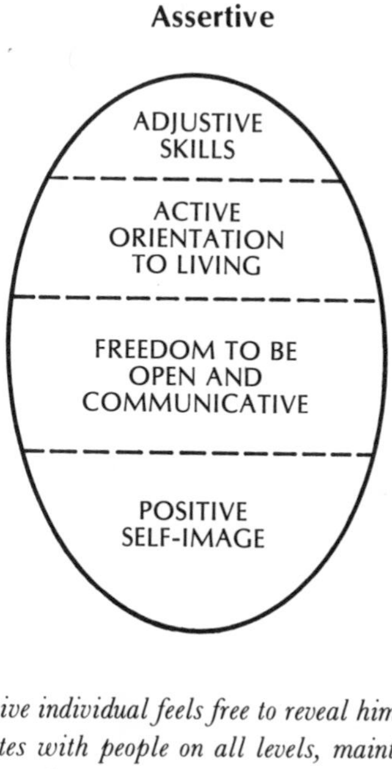
Assertive
ADJUSTIVE SKILLS
ACTIVE ORIENTATION TO LIVING
FREEDOM TO BE OPEN AND COMMUNICATIVE
POSITIVE SELF-IMAGE

The Assertive individual feels free to reveal himself or herself, communicates with people on all levels, maintains an active orientation to living, accepts strengths and limitations, and has an emotional and philosophical "core," or point of view.

situations of stress, frustration, and conflict. Whether you are Assertive, Simple Unassertive, or Manic Concessive depends mainly on how neurotic you are: how much stress you can toler-

Simple Unassertive

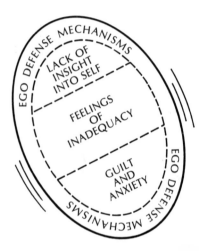

In the Simple Unassertive personality, the "egg" is teetering but retains its structural integrity through ego-defense mechanisms. Right-siding the Simple Unassertive psyche requires a rechanneling of energies spent on defenses into learning new, assertive behaviors.

ate; how much reassurance from others you need to maintain a positive self-image; how high or low your fear and anxiety thresholds are.

As I mentioned before, Assertiveness Training *can* be helpful to Simple Unassertives. They are the neurotics who have the skill to reduce the anxiety produced by conflict or frustration by using ego-defense mechanisms. They can block out their anxiety with a mind-filling ritual or compulsion. They can project or displace their anxiety onto someone else. They can explain it away through rationalization. They can avoid it completely. They can suppress anxiety and turn it into a work of art.

These defense mechanisms are not assertive responses, but they do prevent further erosion of the psyche and foster a basic ability to learn adjustive skills. The Simple Unassertive, then, is likely to be able to learn more difficult, assertive behaviors.

Manic Concessives, on the other hand, lack even the basic ego-defense skills and so are virtually helpless against the constant, gnawing anxiety they feel. They cannot be expected to learn assertive behaviors when they haven't yet mastered the fundamentals of mental survival, as have Simple Unassertives. Manic Concessives do all they can just to ward off anxiety attacks, nervous breakdowns, and psychosis.

Manic Concessive

Characterized by anxiety neurosis (chronic anxiety caused by an obscure or complex source). The Manic Concessive lacks defense mechanisms that could stabilize psyche and reduce anxiety. "Yoke" of "egg" is held together by enormous amounts of positive reinforcement from others, often leading to such severe conditions as alimony.

Case

Jeannie B. was an anal retentive until a major earthquake in 1971 damaged her Los Angeles home and several important defense mechanisms. Over the next five years, Jeannie developed acute anxiety neurosis. Although unable to pinpoint the source of her chronic paranoia, she became nonetheless convinced that "something terrible was going to happen."

For the last year she had felt physically cold all the time. She admitted to running up enormous gas bills "just trying to stay warm." She had every room in the house insulated, had stopped buying frozen foods, and had even covered up the air conditioner with wallpaper. When she felt an anxiety attack coming on, her paranoia would climax. She would run and unplug the refrigerator, which would invariably lead to an argument with her otherwise tolerant husband, Jay, who had "had it up to here" with spoiled cream curdling in his coffee. Jeannie and Jay would fight. Jeannie would scream, "My God, Jay, isn't there enough ice in the world already?" Jay would just shake his head and let her leave it unplugged.

By the time summer came, however, Jay couldn't take it anymore. He brought Jeannie into my office and pleaded with me to "do something." That first meeting was difficult. Jeannie was extremely guarded with me. She wouldn't look me in the eyes. She wouldn't communicate her feelings. She wouldn't even take off her parka and ski goggles. I asked her if she wanted to sit there and shiver or if she wanted to talk her problems out and start leading a fulfilled life. "What's the *use?*" she snapped back. "We're on the verge of another *Ice Age!*"

With the help of psychoanalysis, I discovered the root of Jeannie's fears. What she was really experiencing, I surmised, was a fear of sexual penetration that was causing frigidity. Jay confirmed this with me in private, anxious to confess that as long as they had been married, Jeannie had treated him "like ca-ca from Mars or something" whenever he had tried to get intimate.

I then discovered that Jeannie was the oldest of seven daughters and that, when her mother found out she could have no more children, her domineering and disappointed father promoted her to "son." This put enormous performance pressures on Jeannie, who became a tomboy against her will ("I hated baseball...I still do"), at once identifying with, and fearing, her father. As she approached the dating age, this transformed itself into a fear of men in general, which Jeannie tried desperately to disguise for fear of never finding anyone to marry (all she really wanted).

About a year before she began Concession Training, Jeannie had related her frigidity problems to an orgasm-conscious girl friend, who recommended an Assertiveness Training book that she had read. Jeannie picked up a copy of the book and for two months followed the regimen religiously. But the harder she tried to have orgasms, the more frustrated she became. She would lie on her bed for hours screaming "I want my orgasm!" but nothing ever happened. For Jeannie it was the ultimate failure. She had failed at being a man (for her father), and now she was failing at being a woman.

Ironically, though, the same earthquake that had begun her on a downward spiral into anxiety neurosis had also planted the idea in her mind that natural disasters were great equalizers that made everyone in the community feel equally frightened and insignificant. The day of the earthquake, she remembered, had been the one day when she, and everyone around her, was too preoccupied with fear to focus on her problems and failures. So when the frigidity trauma occurred, Jeannie's subconscious simply invented another natural disaster (impending glacial Ice Age) to make her new, catastrophic sense of worthlessness seem mild by comparison.

Once we had examined the underlying causes of her behavior, Jeannie and I began to talk candidly about her sex life. It became very clear to her what had been going on and what she could do to change her self-concept. First, I got her away from the idea that she *had* to achieve an orgasm—or anything else in this world. I began by chuckling frankly about how absurdly overrated orgasms were, explaining over and over the myth of the vaginal orgasm and citing numerous examples of famous women throughout history who had never had orgasms at all. Within two months Jeannie was chuckling right tations and all, and try to gravitate toward the security and peace of mind that will allow them to survive happily ever after.

tations and all, and try to gravitate toward the security and peace of mind that will allow them to survive happily ever after.

along with me. She even started referring to them as "boregasms."

With her huge performance anxiety reduced, Jeannie was sufficiently at ease to get in touch with her body. Under my direction, she and Jay redid the bedroom in bright, warm colors and then began a daily routine of foreplay only that increased slowly in both time and intensity. For the first week of actual intercourse, I had Jay wear special prophylactics, on which Jeannie would paint little yellow happy faces in the afternoons.

Within six months Jeannie had forgotten all about orgasms and was well on her way toward having one. For the first time in her life she was really enjoying sex. Where she once had a fear of penetration, she now had a voracious appetite for it, wanting her husband every day, morning, noon, and night!

Jay wanted her too, until he became impotent. It seems that as Jeannie's sexual need increased, Jay developed an enormous performance anxiety about not being able to satisfy her. The harder he tried, the worse it got.

By the dead of winter, Jeannie couldn't take it anymore. She brought Jay to the office and pleaded with me to do something.

That meeting was difficult. Jay just stood there in his jogging shorts, repeatedly asking, "Is it hot in here, or is it just me?"

In psychoanalysis Jay revealed many repressed fears, from an obsessive desire to see his nudist mother fully clothed to an edifice complex he had developed on a business trip to New York City.

I began to put Jay at ease with his problem in much the same way as I did Jeannie. I showed him photographs of statues of famous men, none of which had an erect penis. I explained how ancient warriors abstained from intercourse for days, sometimes weeks, before battle, because it sapped their strength and manhood. Finally, I taught Jay how to use sublimation (chapter 3) to create erotic poetry and turn his frustration into something of value.

Following my prescription, Jay began to write erotic poetry and read it to Jeannie at night. He would sit on the bed in a pair of specially made chain-mail briefs, recite the verse, and slowly massage her entire body. After a month, Jay was as turned on as Jeannie. After another month, I allowed him to take off the briefs and continue, still without intercourse.

By the time spring came around, so had Jay. He and Jeannie were once again on the same sexual wavelength, enjoying each other's minds and bodies more than ever.

THE 40-PERCENT SOLUTION[4]

Assertiveness Training looks upon inabilities to set career goals, to be socially mobile, or to handle criticism as prime obstacles to happiness. They are obstacles indeed for Simple Unassertives, whose idea of happiness is a better-paying, higher-stress job; whose secret desire is to be the life of the party; who hunger inside for the admiration they so seldom receive.

But for Manic Concessives, whose idea of happiness is getting sideswiped by someone who has insurance, these inabilities are not obstacles at all. Manic Concessives don't need that higher-stress job. They don't want to be the life of the party. They couldn't care less about coming off assertively in an argument with a stranger. They would be interested just in surviving the mental violence of the argument and making sure it didn't lead to physical violence. Because of the sacred bias, though,

[4]See footnote 2, page 12.

they have learned to feel guilty when points are scored against them, when they are made to look foolish or incompetent. They cannot concentrate on blocking out criticism to stave off anxiety because they are pressured into trying to fight manipulation with manipulation. Having no manipulative skills, they are further defeated and frustrated. By trying to play the other guy's game, which in their heart of hearts they neither want nor need, they are set up for failure time and time again. Their self-image remains shattered.

Concession Training is the solution. It was formulated specifically for Manic Concessives and is thus devoid of condescension and counterproductive goals. It maintains that:

1. Manic Concessives are in a class by themselves. Their deep-seated fear of mental and physical violence cannot be glossed over as simple behavioral deficits.

2. Reducing chronic anxiety by learning certain defense mechanisms, physical exercises, and meditative mantras is the first order of business for every Manic Concessive.

3. Cowardice is not a disease, but rather a very natural survival instinct, and that the only true cowards are those people who will not come to love themselves for what they are, limi-

2
Your Concession Inventory

*Nothing from nothing
leaves nothing.*

WILLIAM PRESTON

Just as no two snowflakes are exactly alike, no two unassertive persons have exactly the same neurotic patterns. Nor are they neurotic to exactly the same degree. This makes it impossible to draw a fine dividing line between Simple Unassertive and Manic Concessive behavior. A person who is Manic Concessive on the job—who feels obligated to keep the coffee area clean, who feels guilty every time the photocopy machine breaks down, who feels devalued by the slightest reprimand from the boss—might be but a Simple Unassertive at home, able to use defense mechanisms on pets or plants and thus discharge pent-up hostility without having to fear physical harm or life-altering trauma (such as being fired from a job).

Even within the Manic Concessive community proper, the intensity of anxiety neurosis varies. While one Manic Concessive might respond to a diffuse paranoia by dead-bolt lock-

37

ing every door and window and activating a burglar-alarm system before going to sleep at night, another might become an insomniac who rests with one eye open and a bazooka trained on the bedroom door.

Still, for the sake of choosing the correct training (AT or CT), it is important for you, the reader, to get an objective, categorical view of your concession tendencies; to measure your coping ability; to find out once and for all where you stand—or kneel—in relation to the world around you.

The following pages contain various tests, the scores of which, when tabulated, will be self-explanatory. If you are worried that someone might find this book with your answers filled in, transcribe your answers on a separate piece of paper. If you are worried that someone may find the piece of paper, dispose of it immediately after the tabulation.

Whatever you do, try to relax. Take a few deep breaths and try to answer the questions as honestly as you possibly can.

UPTIGHT LOWDOWN

This checklist helps you measure your fear and anxiety thresholds. Listed are stimuli and situations common to our lives. Each is followed by a choice (a, b, c, or d) corresponding to the degree of uptightness you experience responding to that stimulus or situation.

Circle either (a) "Doesn't bother me at all," (b) "Bothers me a little," (c) "Bothers me a lot," or (d) "Anything but that!"

1. SPEAKING IN FRONT OF FIFTY PEOPLE

   a   b   c   d

2. A STRANGER WALKING TOWARD YOU AT NIGHT

   a   b   c   d

3. MAKING EYE CONTACT WITH A STRANGER IN AN ELEVATOR

   a   b   c   d

4. STARTING A CONVERSATION WITH A STRANGER

   a   b   c   d

5. A LULL IN THE CONVERSATION WITH A STRANGER

   a   b   c   d

6. WATCHING A FISTFIGHT ERUPT BETWEEN TWO STRANGERS

   a   b   c   ╱ d

7. PICKING UP MALE HITCHHIKERS

   a   b   c   d ╱

8. USING THE SELF-SERVE PUMP AT A GAS STATION

   a ╱   b   c   d

9. STALLING IN THE MIDDLE OF AN INTERSECTION

   a   b   c ╱ d

10. DRIVING PAST THE SCENE OF A HEAD-ON COLLISION

    a   b   c   ╱ d

11. USING A CROWDED PUBLIC RESTROOM

    a ᴧ   b   c   d

12. ASKING FOR A FIRST DATE

    a   b   c ╱ d

13. ASKING YOUR BOSS FOR A RAISE

    a   b   c   d

14. GOING ON A JOB INTERVIEW

    a   b   c   d

15. GOING TO A MOVIE ALONE

    a   b   c   d

16. HAVING A CAVITY FILLED

    a   b   c   d

17. HAVING TO SERVE ON A JURY

    a   b   c   d

18. FLYING IN AN AIRPLANE

    a   b   c   d

19. BEING IGNORED

    a   b   c   d

20. BEING THE CENTER OF ATTENTION

    a   b   c   d

21. EXPRESSING ANGER

    a   b   c   d

22. ADMITTING WEAKNESSES

    a   b   c   d

23. SAYING "I'M SORRY"

    a   b   c   d

24. BEING ROMANTIC

    a   b   c   d

25. BEING SEXUALLY AGGRESSIVE

    a   b   c   d

26. WEARING A BATHING SUIT IN PUBLIC

    a   b   c   d

27. BEING NAKED IN FRONT OF FRIENDS OF THE SAME SEX

    a   b   c   d

28. BEING NAKED IN PRIVATE

    a   b   c   d

29. RECEIVING CRITICISM

       a   b   c   d

30. RECEIVING A COMPLIMENT

       a   b   c   d

31. KNOWING THAT YOU WILL DIE SOMEDAY

       a   b   c   d

CONFLICT RESPONSE

The tranquillity of our lives is constantly disrupted by conflict situations which force us to respond in some definitive manner. Following is a series of situations you may have faced already or could face at some time in your life.

After reading the situation, circle the answer (a, b, c, or d) that most closely resembles the kind of response you would make.

32. YOU'RE WORKING OVERTIME AT THE OFFICE AGAIN TONIGHT. THREE THUGS BREAK THROUGH THE DOOR, DEMAND YOUR MONEY, AND THREATEN TO KILL YOU. YOUR IMMEDIATE REACTION WOULD BE TO:

   (a) Rip the blade off the paper cutter and start slashing away at their faces.

    (b) Make a mad dash for the telephone to call the police.

    (c) Give them your money and try to reason with them about your life.

    (d) Slash the telephone cord in a show of good faith, hand over your money, and then faint.

33. YOU'RE BY YOURSELF AT A RATHER DULL PARTY. SUDDENLY, YOU HEAR A GROUP OF PEOPLE BEGIN LAUGHING UPROARIOUSLY. YOU WOULD PROBABLY:

    (a) Gravitate toward the laughter and introduce yourself.

    (b) Gravitate toward the laughter and hope someone introduces himself.

    (c) Try to decide if you feel like gravitating toward the laughter.

    (d) Pray that their laughing at you doesn't lead to physical harassment.

34. SOMEONE STEALS THE PARKING SPACE YOU WERE GETTING READY TO BACK INTO. YOUR RESPONSE WOULD BE TO:

    (a) Jump out of your car, start a fistfight with the driver of the other car, and ask questions later.

(b) Open your door, look back, and yell, "Hey, that's *my* space, buddy!"

(c) Grumble that it's your space and drive on.

(d) Jump out of your car, open the hood, pretend that you're just stopping to check the battery fluid, smile, jump back in the car, and drive on.

35. BEFORE AN INTERSECTION WITH NO SIGNAL, YOU'RE WAITING TO MAKE A LEFT TURN INTO HEAVY TWO-WAY TRAFFIC. CARS ARE PILING UP BEHIND YOU. STILL NO BREAK IN THE TRAFFIC. THE CAR BEHIND YOU STARTS HONKING. YOU WOULD MOST LIKELY:

(a) Scream an obscenity out the window, throw it into reverse, and bash out his headlights.

(b) Grumble some obscenity under your breath and slowly inch your car forward.

(c) Jerk the car forward, giving him a penitant wave of the hand.

(d) I never make left turns without a signal. I always make three right turns instead.

36. YOU'RE AT A PARTY WITH YOUR GIRL FRIEND. A DRUNK TEAMSTER FROM A BROKEN HOME APPROACHES AND STARTS RUBBING HER BREASTS. YOU WOULD PROBABLY:

    (a) Just beat the holy @#!*[5] out of him right then and there.
    (b) Push his hands away, then "choose him off."
    (c) Grab your girl friend, leave in a huff, and yell at her for leading the guy on.
    (d) Start apologizing for the size of her breasts.

37. A MECHANIC HANDS YOU A $268 BILL FOR A MAJOR TUNE-UP AND AN OIL CHANGE. WITHOUT HESITATION YOU WOULD:

    (a) Tear the bill up in his face, rip the keys out of his hand, and drive away.
    (b) Demand to see the service manager for a full accounting of the work.
    (c) Call your dad for advice.
    (d) Write him a check for $268, commenting that "an ounce of prevention is worth a pound of cure."

[5] Shit.

38. YOU'RE HOME IN BED WITH A TERRIBLE COLD. ONE OF YOUR BOSSES CALLS TO SAY THAT IF YOU GET ANOTHER EXCELLENT SUMMARY PLAN DESCRIPTION OUT WITHIN TWO WEEKS, SHE'S GOING TO PROMOTE YOU TO SUPERVISOR OF YOUR ENTIRE DEPARTMENT. YOU WOULD PROBABLY:

(a) Bundle up, dump a handful of Vitamin C, and go back in to work.
(b) Have a friend from work drop off some of your notes so that you can start writing.
(c) Start worrying that if your cold gets any worse, you won't be able to write and you won't become supervisor.
(d) Try to catch pneumonia, so you won't have to become supervisor.

39. YOU COME HOME EARLY FOR DINNER ONE NIGHT AND FIND YOUR LOVER IN BED WITH ANOTHER. INSTINCTIVELY YOU WOULD:

(a) Grab a gun and start blamming away at their loins.
(b) Chase the new lover out of the house and then rough up your mate.
(c) Say something terribly sarcastic to your mate and then storm out.

(d) Rush back to the market to pick up another steak.

40. YOU'RE AT A GOOD RESTAURANT WITH A DATE. YOU SUDDENLY DISCOVER A DEAD FLY IN YOUR RICE PILAF. YOU WOULD IMMEDIATELY:

(a) Start yelling for the waiter, make a big scene, grab your date, and leave cursing.

(b) Summon the waiter, show him the fly, tell him that you're appalled and won't pay for either meal, and then leave, quietly disgusted.

(c) Show the fly to your date, hoping she'll take the initiative, since you hate to make a scene.

(d) Hide the fly before your date can see it and embarrass you by making a scene.

41. YOUR SISTER HAS JUST TOLD YOU THAT SHE'S IN LOVE WITH A MAN OF ANOTHER RACE AND RELIGION, THAT SHE'S PREGNANT BY HIM, AND THAT SHE'S GOING TO MARRY HIM IN TWO WEEKS. YOUR BIGGEST CONCERN WOULD BE:

(a) The emotional effect on your family.

(b) The psychological effect on the child.

(c) The reaction of your friends.

(d) Having to get a date for the wedding.

42. A GOOD FRIEND BORROWED $50 FROM YOU "'TIL TOMORROW." IT'S BEEN TWO WEEKS NOW, AND YOU NEED THAT MONEY BACK TO PAY YOUR RENT! WHAT WOULD YOU DO?

   (a) I woulda been on his case *last* week and gotten paid back.
   (b) I'd simply call him up and tell him that I really need that money back so I can pay my rent.
   (c) I'd broach the subject in conversation with something like, "Say, how are you fixed for funds these days, anyway?"
   (d) I'd borrow $50 from my folks (good friends are hard to find!).

43. YOU'RE AT A MOVIE THEATER. SOME WISE GUY BEHIND YOU WON'T KEEP QUIET. CHANCES ARE YOU WOULD:

   (a) Turn around and tell him that if you hear one more peep, his ass is grass.
   (b) Turn around and ask him to please shut up.
   (c) Get up, report him to the usher, and change seats.
   (d) Get up, tell him you'll be right back, and change theaters.

44. IN A WARTIME COMBAT SITUATION, YOU WOULD BE MOST EFFECTIVE AS:

    (a) A front-line infantryman.
    (b) A fighter pilot or bombardier.
    (c) A medic.
    (d) A comic in the USO show.

45. WHICH OF THE FOLLOWING SIGHTS WOULD NOT MAKE YOU SQUEAMISH?

    (a) A field trip to a slaughterhouse.
    (b) An aborigine throwing up on your chest.
    (c) Melted ice cream on the sidewalk.
    (d) None of the above.

46. IF YOU FEEL STRONGLY ABOUT A CONTROVERSIAL POLITICAL ISSUE, WILL YOU PUT A BUMPER STICKER ON YOUR CAR?

    (a) Hell, yes, probably two or three of 'em!
    (b) Yes.
    (c) No—well, I *would,* but you just can't get that glue stuff off your bumper, and anyway my vote's what really counts.
    (d) No, because I never feel strongly.

47. WHILE GETTING READY FOR BED, YOU NOTICE A VERY LARGE SPIDER CRAWLING ALONG THE

WALL ONE FOOT ABOVE YOUR MATTRESS. YOU
WOULD PROBABLY:

(a) Smash it with your palm.
(b) Trap it with a wadded tissue and dispose of it.
(c) Skewer it with a broom and dispose of it.
(d) Spray it with furniture wax until it stopped, then hang a picture over it.

GUILT BY ASSOCIATION

The way we perceive abstract or unusual visual forms reveals the preoccupations of our subconscious mind. Following are three visual forms, each followed by four possible answers. Circle the answer (a, b, c, or d) which is closest to what you perceived the form to be at first glance.

48. WHAT DO YOU SEE IN THE FORM BELOW?

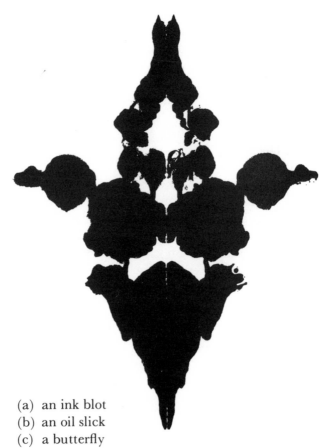

(a) an ink blot
(b) an oil slick
(c) a butterfly
(d) an Arab terrorist

49. WHAT DO YOU SEE IN THE OPTICAL ILLUSION
BELOW?

(a) a vase
(b) two faces
(c) a vase *and* two faces
(d) a goblet of poison

50. WHAT DOES THE LINE DRAWING BELOW MAKE YOU THINK OF?

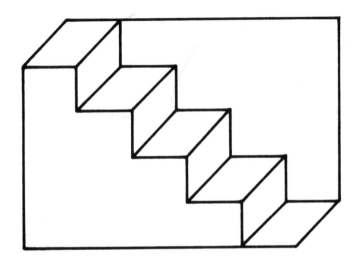

(a) a staircase
(b) an upside-down staircase
(c) a staircase *and* an upside-down staircase
(d) falling down a staircase

TABULATING YOUR SCORE

Each a answer is worth 4 points, each b answer 3 points, each c answer 2 points, and each d answer 1 point. Go back, count up your total points, then refer to the chart below to find your classification.

If your score was 50–89 points	You are a MANIC CONCESSIVE
If your score was 90–139 points	You are a SIMPLE UNASSERTIVE
If your score was 140–179 points	You are an ASSERTIVE person
If your score was 180–205	You are an AGGRESSIVE person

If you are a Manic Concessive, Concession Training techniques will help you reduce anxiety, increase your stress tolerance, and learn to love yourself and accept your limitations.

If you are a Simple Unassertive, you have probably mastered a few anxiety-reducing defense mechanisms and possess enough adjustive skill to try your hand at Assertiveness Training. Do *not,* however, let an AT handbook suffice. Enroll in Assertiveness Training workshops or private therapy sessions. (If you scored in the 90s, you may be a "closet concessive." Try Concession Training for three months and then take the tests again.)

If you are an assertive person, you probably don't need therapy. You probably have a steady mate, a few close friends, a job you're happy with, realistic goals, and an active orientation to living. Be careful, though. Any sudden, unexpected life trauma such as death or an income tax audit could send you into one of the two previous catagories.

If you are an extremely *aggressive person,* you definitely don't need therapy. What you need is surgery, preferably a prefrontal lobotomy. Anything to keep you strapped down and out of the mainstream of civilized society. It's animals like you who make life miserable for the rest of us![6]

[6]Oh, you want rehabilitation? Great, why don't you strap yourself to an offshore drilling platform in the North Sea for a long winter? Maybe you'll begin to understand the constant chill that your prey experiences knowing you're out there. If it weren't for subspecies like you, Manic Concessives could live in peace and dignity!

3
Don't Say Yes When You Want to Say Yes, Sir!—Techniques of Concession Training

*Better is a little
with Content,
than much with Contention.*

BENJAMIN FRANKLIN

YOUR MANIC CONCESSIVE BILL OF RIGHTS

I. YOU HAVE THE RIGHT TO REMAIN SILENT.

II. YOU HAVE THE RIGHT TO CHANGE YOUR MIND.

III. YOU HAVE THE RIGHT TO OFFER NO REASONS OR EXCUSES FOR YOUR COWARDICE, UNLESS THE QUESTIONER IS VIOLENCE-PRONE.

IV. YOU HAVE THE RIGHT TO AVOID, SUPPRESS, OR RATIONALIZE ANY ANXIETY OR SOURCE OF ANXIETY.

V. YOU HAVE THE RIGHT TO BE ILLOGICAL, CONTRADICTORY, AND CIRCUMLOCUTIOUS.

VI. YOU HAVE THE RIGHT TO RUN, TO HIDE, TO WHIMPER, TO CRY, TO MOPE, AND TO POUT.

VII. YOU HAVE THE RIGHT TO FLATTER, CAJOLE, AND KISS ASS.

VIII. YOU HAVE THE RIGHT TO TAKE NO FOR AN ANSWER.

IX. YOU HAVE THE RIGHT TO LOVE YOURSELF FOR WHAT YOU ARE.

X. YOU HAVE THE RIGHT TO STOP TRYING TO ASSERT YOURSELF AND START LIVING!

CONCESSION TRAINING DEFENSE MECHANISMS

As I noted earlier, the primary goal of Concession Training is to help you stabilize your psyche and reduce chronic paranoia and anxiety. The first step is learning some of the same defense mechanisms that Simple Unassertives use to keep their self-concepts from deteriorating, raise their fear and anxiety thresholds, and avoid sources and situations of stress and frustration.

Avoidance

Since conflicts that could lead to mental or physical violence are a major source of anxiety, you must learn how to avoid conflicts by learning to avoid the types of people who love to instigate them and the kinds of places where these people are most often found.

Early detection of predators in a social situation requires a knowledge of basic physiognomy and behavioral cues. Fortunately, aggressive persons give away their violent tendencies through body language: the way they sit, the way they walk, the gestures they use, their tone of voice, and their facial expressions.

Once you master the fine points of this perceptual language, you will drastically lessen the chance of entering into a conflict situation which could lead to verbal abuse or death.

Look at the following photographs. See if your early warning system can detect the intentions of the two people pictured.

Are his eyes communicating anything to you? Does he look sad? Perplexed? Perturbed?

Are his tense facial muscles telling you that he's in pain? That he's uptight? That he's mongoloid?

Is his flamboyant gesture a cry for help? Attention? Blood?

Does her reaction to meeting you seem inappropriate? Insincere? Hostile?

Is her cigarette smoking hiding a basic insecurity?

Is her shrill laughter really a sexual cue that she wants you?

Is it any consolation to you at this point?

People you should avoid. Avoid anyone who might make you anxious or afraid. Don't go out with any man who has dried food in his beard, or whose toenails are painted black with white crescent moons on them. Tell any woman whose pubis is painted blue to resemble the Bermuda Triangle that you'll "keep in touch." Avoid anyone who has been fried out by psychedelic drugs. If he or she is a former acquaintance, wait just long enough to hear again the story about how he or she took more and more acid every day in order to see God and then finally one day God appeared and said, "Stop taking so much acid," and excuse yourself. Avoid alcoholics. Avoid religious fanatics and recent graduates of est. They're so caught up in their newfound self-image, and their hatred of their old one, that they'll bombard you with endless sermons about how sinful you are, or rake your delicate psyche over the coals in aggressive "sensitivity sessions."

Avoid people with tattoos. Nearly 72 percent of all convicts in U.S. prisons have tattoos (nearly 68 percent above the national average)! Also, watch for signs of negligence in personal hygiene: greasy hair, tooth decay, excessive body odor, and dried sweat rings under the arms. Avoid flashy dressers. They're usually hyperactive, cynical people who tend toward mental violence as a form of recreation.

Avoid adventurous, outdoorsy people. The last thing you need is to get talked into a dangerous ski trip or backpacking jaunt into the wilderness. Avoid anyone who drives aggressively on the road. Keep people from tailgaiting you with a bumper sticker that says "Warning: I Brake for Insects!" If you have the money, buy a car like those used by your local police department. Have it painted a similar color and put a large antenna on the trunk. People will tend to slow down to a safer speed the moment they spot you coming.

Avoid overachievers: people who finish term papers or reports two weeks before they're due, people who can't decide between medical school and law school, people whose biggest worry is being forced into a higher tax bracket next year. Associating with overachievers can only make you feel like an underachiever. They'll nod affirmatively during everything you say until you're finished, at which point they'll shake their heads no or grin in condescending tolerance of your "nice try" at making a point. Their constant patronization is designed to keep you around, because you're a good audience and because you marvel at their achievements. All they do for you, in the long run, is increase your feelings of inferiority.

Similarly, avoid developing friendships with likable hulks. While their physical prowess might give you a feeling of security, hulks tend to freely invite themselves (and you) into violent confrontations. Often it's two-on-two. You could get hurt. If you want to feel protected, find the money and hire a professional bodyguard. He'll do the job without imposing friendship.

Finally, avoid salespersons or other strangers who might come to your house or apartment. Put a red quarantine sign on your door, keep an un-listed phone number, and install an answering device on your telephone with a recording that says: "I'm sorry, the person you have reached is not in service at this time. Please leave your name and a brief encouraging message."

Places you should avoid. Avoid any place where aggressive persons congregate. Avoid any bar that is not part of a large restaurant or hotel. Small bars attract small minds, who are there to drink, spread their melancholy, and, often, release pent-up rage with pool cues and broken bottles. Even in a large bar, you should keep one ear open for anyone who is becoming bois-terous or giving the waitress a hard time. If you notice this happening, don't stare at the person!

Just finish your soft drink and leave. On the way home, make sure to avoid other favorite loitering spots of predators: street corners, alleys, dimly lit parking lots, all-night food stands, and liquor stores.

Avoid major sporting events. There are more aggressive persons per square yard at certain sporting events than at a gangland funeral. Consider the pleasure of watching sports at home on television: seeing all those instant replays and close-ups of the action, listening to the engaging commentary of a professional announcer, grabbing a snack without having to wait in a line full of strangers. If you *must* attend a sporting event, buy the most expensive seats you can afford. You'll almost always be assured of sitting with the most polite and civilized people there.

Avoid hard-rock concerts. Unfortunately, there is no guarantee that the long-haired youth standing or sitting next to you is a mellow, guitar-strumming pacifist. Hard rock attracts hard-core neanderthals, shiftless punks, and decibel junkies who could explode at any minute into crazed fits of ecstasy or violence.

Finally, avoid the temptation to move to a small town. Like many Manic Concessives, you may develop a "Mayberry fantasy" and decide that the solution to your chronic paranoia is to move into the peaceful, friendly, laid-back atmosphere of the country. You'll soon discover, though, that where you were a frightened but happily anonymous recluse in the big city, you are now the frightened talk of the town! Everybody from the mayor to the waitress at the local café is gossiping about that quiet, loner type who just moved in and speculating about your intentions. Before long, you've developed a "Boo Radley complex." Neighborhood kids are tossing pebbles at your windows and daring each other to run up and touch your door. Within two months the entire community is worried that some Sunday you're going to climb the church steeple and open fire with a shotgun. Before you know it, a vigilante committee of Simple Unassertives has drummed you out of town!

Rationalization

Imagine pre-ancient China. One million years ago. A cold, crisp evening during the Ugh Dynasty. Peking man and a few friends are gathered together before the glow of a hot,

white fire,[7] celebrating the kill of a plains an-
telope. Suddenly, the dancing and laughter are
broken by silence. There seems all around to be
a rumbling that builds into a terrific roar. The
group's puzzlement turns to fright. As the roar
breaks through the surface, violent shaking begins. They are terrified and screaming. For
more than a minute (although it probably
seems much longer to them) they experience
the trauma of their lives. The very earth which
is their reference—the very cave which is their
womb—has turned on them. A great, unknowable force has flung its fury against them. The
cave floor shakes and cracks. The walls and ceiling begin to fall. A young girl and a baby are
buried in the rain of falling rock. An old man
who manages to escape the cave falls dead of a
heart seizure. The community's sense of help-
lessness leads to a panic and frenzy resembling
an anxiety attack.

For a week following the tragedy, their anxiety is constantly heightened by aftershocks. Although most survive, they carry the scars of the
experience throughout their lives. Until they
can somehow know and explain the reason for

[7] Fire has grown perceptibly dimmer (yellower) in the
last million years.

this violence, they will exhibit the same disorganization of psyche common among later-day
anxiety neurotics.

Building a rational explanation for seemingly
irrational sources of stress and trauma is one of
the ways man learned to survive. Along with his
ability to adapt to his physical environment, to
outwit food animals which possessed superior
speed and agility, there came necessarily an instinct for rationalization. This allowed man to
keep his psyche intact in the face of unexplain-
able and threatening occurrences.

By organizing his fears, by constructing a rational concept of his universe complete with
deities, deity legends, and deity curio shops, he
could logically explain such "irrational" disasters as earthquakes, floods, and volcanic erup-
tions (punishment), as well as such phenomena
as eclipses, meteor showers, and comets
(omens). By giving his deities such human
character traits as moodiness, pride, and revenge, he could rationalize why these traumatic
events would continue to take place.

Manic Concessives also suffer from chronic
anxiety caused by an obscure and unknowable
source. Reducing this anxiety requires, as in the
case of early man, an organizing of fears
through the construction of a rationale. By

identifying an anxiety source out of his control, by placing the blame for his condition on real or contrived aggressors, the Manic Concessive can rationalize many of his anxieties, short-comings, and outright failures.

Astrology. As man grew more intelligent and socialized, he necessarily developed more so-phisticated forms of rationalization. One form, astrology, is still used by millions to reduce anx-iety and soften blows to the goals.

The beauty part of this "secular Calvinism" is the concept of predestination, the idea that the major determinant of our fate is the posi-tion of planets relative to the backdrop of stel-lar constellations as viewed from the earth at the moment of birth. Unlike the disciplines of Judaism, Buddhism, and Christianity, which teach that individuals create and are respon-sible for their actions, astrology teaches "prefab karma," the idea that our personality traits are predetermined and our behaviors, successes, and failures are continually redetermined by cosmic variables out of our control (and there-fore, out of our responsibility).

Following astrology, the Manic Concessive can win either way. A forecast that brings good news (health, happiness, or success) lifts the spirits, instills hope, and thus reduces anxiety.

A forecast that brings bad news provides celestial excuses which can be used to rationalize shortcomings, failures, or conflict avoidance.

Science or sham, accurate or inaccurate, astrology *works!* It will help you shift the burden of decisiveness and karmic responsibility to a complex, ever-changing set of celestial deities, and, in the process, substantially reduce your anxiety.

Verbal rationalizations. To help you further organize your fears, I've organized a list of age-old tried-and-true rationalizations. When failure in love or life threatens your psychic integration, defend yourself by rationalizing that it wasn't your fault, that it doesn't much matter, or that the worst may really be for the better.

Commit the following phrases to memory and start using them liberally:

Winning isn't everything.
You can't win 'em all.
You win some, you lose some.
Easy come, easy go.
It's not whether you win or lose, it's how you play the game.
Success never comes easy.
It takes ten years to become an overnight success.
I'm just ahead of my time.

The darkest hour is just before the dawn.
Every cloud has a silver lining.
It can only get better.
I've seen worse.
To err is human.
Everybody makes mistakes.
Nobody's perfect.
It happens to the best of us.
It just wasn't my day.
There's always next year.
There's no use crying over spilt milk.
Who needs it?
It's more trouble than it's worth.
I wouldn't take it if they *gave* it away.
Money isn't everything.
I've got my health.
You're as young as you feel.
Chalk it up to experience.
You live and learn.
If you've seen one, you've seen 'em all.
If you can't beat 'em, join 'em.
Just leave well enough alone.
You can't fight city hall.
A bird in the hand is worth two in the bush.
I'd rather reign in hell than serve in heaven.
I'd rather be Red than dead.
I've got enough problems of my own.
Am I my brother's keeper?

Look, I do what I can.

Everybody does it.

If I hadn't, somebody else would have.

He's (she's) not the only starfish in the sea.

She (he) wasn't good enough for me anyway.

Women are all alike.

Men are all alike.

Beauty's only skin deep.

Men only have one thing on their minds.

Better to have loved and lost than never to
have loved at all.

She (he) doesn't know what she's (he's)
missing.

They deserve each other.

It just wasn't in the cards.

Dynamite comes in small packages.

Still water runs deep.

Quality, not quantity.

It's probably a blessing in disguise.

Different strokes for different folks.

Suppression and Sublimation

"Poetry," T. S. Eliot said, "results not from
the expression of emotion, but from the suppression of emotion."

For centuries artists have depended on suppression and sublimation to heat the black coal

of neurosis and turn it into diamonds of creative insight. Salvador Dali, surrealism's enfant terrible, gives much of the credit for his artistic success to these defense mechanisms. They have allowed him to keep his sanity while producing hallucinogenic images of paranoiac reality befitting a true psychotic. In Dali's own words, "The only difference between me and a madman is that *I* am not mad!"

Cursed by an oversensitivity to stress and exaggerated fears of physical pain and death, the young Dali taught himself how to refuse anxiety admittance into his conscious mind. He developed an enormous intellect, a pompous, esoteric vocabulary, and an inordinate distaste for anything "romantic." Thus, he succeeded in insulating his conscious mind from anxiety-producing stimuli, making himself virtually emotion-proof in the face of trauma. This not only kept him from going mad, it pushed all his anxiety into the subconscious mind, the only place where it can have any aesthetic value. He then, in addition to his painterly skills, developed the "paranoid-critical activity," a creative frenzy resembling an anxiety attack. Through the paranoid-critical activity he periodically experienced all at once the monstrous fears he had been suppressing. In a trancelike state he began furiously creating, transferring the built-up mental sewage to canvas, where it was transformed into art!

Manic Concessives with even the slightest creative abilities can use suppression to focus their experience of debilitating anxiety: keeping it under control to subsidize the business of living, flushing it out to produce something of lasting value, relegating it to the subconscious, where it is manageable. Here are three techniques.

1. Build an intellect like a fortress. Start with a euphemistic vocabulary. By using sophisticated, pleasant-sounding synonyms for the common words we use to describe unpleasant stimuli, you make your conscious mind less sensitive to those stimuli and, ultimately, less vulnerable to the anxiety they produce. Learn to substitute "paranoid" for scared, "pugnacious" for violence-prone, "truculent" for cruel, "brouhaha" for fight, "cudgel" for beat, "garrote" for strangle, "dispatch" for kill, "departed" for dead, "polemic" for argument, "vituperation" for abuse, "travail" for anguish, "flaccid" for limp, "gelid" for frigid, and "seismism" for earthquake. Use "abandon" only as a noun. Increase your general intellectuality by working such words into your vocabulary as albeit, altruism, anachronism, bromide, coitus, conundrum, dichotomy, feign, innocuous, invidious, libertine, licentious, livid, matriculate, mawkish, modicum, prevaricate, ribald, saccharine, saturnine, and volatile.

Next, audit community college courses in philosophy. By auditing the classes, you'll avoid the trauma that comes with tests, grades, and peer pressure. And, as you learn, you'll begin to view the world very coolly, as a compilation of ideas, abstractions, and statistics. Before long you'll be able to elevate to rational explanation any source or potential source of anxiety.

2. Keep a dream diary. Remember, although intellectualization is keeping anxiety from your conscious mind, it is being impacted in your subconscious mind and must be flushed out periodically. The key is your dream life, where frustrations and fears appear as convoluted scenarios and bizarre images. These dreams will become the resource material for your artistic creations, so log them well! Keep either a diary or a cassette tape recorder handy near your bed. Each morning, mumble or scribble down the images from your dreams. Make comprehensive notes on any particularly odd images, because, no matter what you might think at the time, you won't remember them later in any detail.

3. Start creating! Choose any medium that suits you: painting, drawing, sculpture, poetry, prose, or music. When you feel an anxiety attack coming on, instead of becoming its victim, become its master by immediately referring to your dream diary. Scour the images while you feel the anxiety and pain. Start creating. Let those suppressed fears come through. Experience them deeply for the moment, and you'll exorcise them from your conscious life. When the attack passes, you'll feel relieved, and you'll have something that is truly worthwhile to show for it. You'll be a bona fide suffering artist, and you'll reduce the amount of free-floating anxiety in your life by at least 50 percent. Before long you'll gain almost complete control over when and where you have your anxiety attacks, being able to summon them up on command, just like the great masters!

If you're a Manic Concessive with a history of sexual problems, you can use sublimation in the same way, to turn those "deviant" impulses and catastrophic frustrations into socially acceptable artistic expression. Unlike masturbation, sublimation results in the creation of something tangible and lasting—something that can be respected and enjoyed long after the cretin glee of self-abuse has subsided.

This is particularly relevant, considering the severe forms of frigidity and impotence that Manic Concessives experience:

	ASSERTIVE	SIMPLE UNASSERTIVE	MANIC CONCESSIVE
M A L E	Achieves full erection and subsequent orgasm	Penis remains flaccid or partially erect	Knob of penis actually begins to recede into foreskin
F E M A L E	Vagina loosens and secretes lubricant, vulva becomes wet	Vagina remains tight, vulva remains dry	Vagina actually begins to secrete Spackle

Of course, it would be naïve to assume that sublimation can reverse impotence or frigidity. It can, however, particularly because of the massive intellectualization, substantially lessen the *desire* for sexual activity (see accompanying graph). Whatever frustration remains can be turned into erotic art.

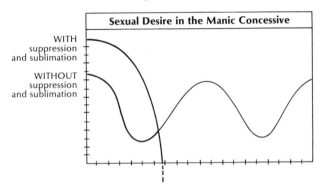

CONCESSION TRAINING EXERCISES

How many hockey players cower at the thought of rough physical contact? How many baseball players are too embarrassed to spit in public? When was the last time a football game was stopped because the linebacker was having an anxiety attack?

Why is it that people who regularly engage in intense physical activity seem to be less anxious and more "together" than those who don't? The answer is simple. Strenuous physical exercise releases tension, builds confidence in the body, and helps keep cerebral preoccupations in perspective.

Some Manic Concessives dive full speed ahead into suppression and sublimation techniques, forgetting that any strenuous intellectualization must be counterbalanced with strenuous exercise. They begin to experience "mind-body drift." The more cerebral they become, the more they live in the insulated world of ideas, the less sensitive they become to the needs of their bodies. They begin to see their bodies as mere mediums for their minds, as mere vehicles for stimulation. Because there is more immediate gratification in food, alcohol, or marijuana than there is in sweating, they become locked into a self-indulgent spiral that produces a body oversensitive to pain, disease, and stress. As a result, they lose confidence both in the way they look (self-image) and in their ability to perform in situations of conflict (outrunning an aggressor).

As obvious as the prescription might seem, getting a daily diet of intense physical activity is not easy for the Manic Concessive. Most MCs shy away from sports that involve physical contact. In fact, most avoid sports that involve any *personal* contact. Even jogging involves serious compromise in the real world: traffic, stray dogs, irate pedestrians, etc.

With these reservations in mind, I've designed a series of three strenuous physical exercises that you can perform every day, in the privacy of your own room.

Pushovers

Position 1   Position 2

A helpful exercise if you're uptight about your sexuality, but even more uptight about failing to find a mate or being thought of as a prude. Pushovers invigorate the pelvic muscles, relax the entire body, and help desensitize you to the "nasty" feeling of a sensual, suggestive posture. They help you learn to give in sexually and feel good about it!

Alternate between positions 1 and 2 every 5 seconds for 3 minutes, three times a day.

Jumbo Jacks

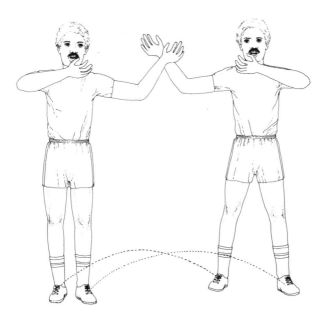

Position 1   Position 2

This late-night exercise is a substitute for junk-food over-dosing. Instead of stuffing your mouth with surrogate love, just go through the motions instead, as you exercise the biceps, calves, and thighs, and the mandible muscles of the mouth. After 10 minutes of Jumbo Jacks you'll be exhausted. You won't feel hungry (exercise shrinks the stomach muscles), and you'll be ready for a peaceful, uninterrupted night's rest.

The Triple Kowtow[8]

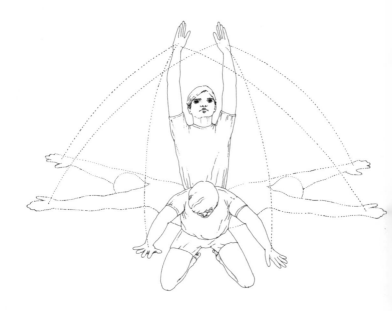

The Triple Kowtow helps you learn to feel more comfortable with your concession while you take unwanted inches off the stomach, stretch the muscles of the lower back, and completely relax the spine.

Repeat 3 positions continually for 10 minutes, 3 times a day.

[8]Not to be confused with the Triple Salchow of figure skating.

CONCESSION TRAINING MANTRAS

We're all familiar with the soothing, hypnotic effect that a mother's lullaby has on a restless child. The sweet melody blends with the rhythmic, almost monotonous lyric cadence to relax the child completely, allowing its mind and body to be seduced by sleep.

Chanting in meditation, used for centuries by holy persons around the world, works on the same basic principle. By repeating over and over a prescribed mantra, or lullaby, one can achieve a state of inner calm, resulting in decreased muscle tension and increased mental discipline and self-actualization.

You can use this form of autosuggestion to reduce anxiety and to reaffirm the basic precepts of Concession Training. By chanting one or all of the following mantras for 10 to 15 minutes twice a day, you'll feel better about yourself, your position in life, and your ability to cope with situations of conflict and frustration.

"Nam, Yoko, Ringo, Kilo"

Remembering good times and past glories can actually strengthen the psyche by helping you to forget, if only for a time, the quagmire of crises and cover-ups that have come to characterize your concessive conscious. Many siblings from the sixties chant "Nam, Yoko, Ringo, Kilo" to escape into the memories of the simpler, more exciting, more wondrous days of youth. Beyond its calming effect, this quadrastew of images has a "phonetics of purpose"—a didactic dimension reminding you that you have great memories to survive for, to live for, to try to reconstruct again. As you repeat the chant, feel your body tension dissipating. Feel the fun of those sock hops returning. Feel the total freedom and lack of responsibility. When you're refreshed, come out of the trance and smile!

"Oh, God, Please Make Them Leave Me Alone!"

Assume a crouching position, teeth chattering, eyes shut. Try to recall or imagine a scene of physical violence which is threatening you. See the aggressor's face. Don't block it out. Even if the images are painful, keep chanting. Look long and hard into his face. See the terrorism in his eyes, the scars on his forehead. Feel yourself swelling with fear. Feel yourself wanting to vomit. Begin breathing in huge, short gasps. Feel the trembling now. Move *inside* the trembling. Become *one* with the trembling and the fear. Realize that statistics have finally caught up with you. Feel your skin being slashed, your flesh being torn. Know that all that matters about your beautiful face now is the tensile strength of that bone casing. Feel the pain, the delirious, gut-wrenching fear of death. Let it seize you and become you. See yourself bloody and screaming for help. Get behind the scream. *Become* the scream!

Now stop. Open one eye and look from side to side. Keep chanting. Realize that your scream has scared off the aggressor. Realize that God has answered your prayers, that the aggressor has gone, that you are wounded but will heal. Feel the sympathy of friends and strangers alike. Smell the flowers in your hospital room. Enjoy the sympathy. Feel yourself healing up good as new. See yourself winking at the doctor or nurse as you leave the hospital. Feel yourself returning to a normal life, calm and relieved.

"Oh, God, please make them leave me alone!" desensitizes you to the chronic anxiety you experience contemplating physical violence. Having allowed yourself to really feel the fear, to experience it deeply, you move *beyond* it. Whatever common stress you might encounter the remainder of the day will probably seem mild by comparison. Chances are, you'll be able to take it in stride!

"Sticks and Stones May Break My Bones, but Names Will Never Hurt Me!"

The wisdom beneath this childhood chant helps desensitize you to mental violence. Use this mantra in any social situation where an aggressor is creating anxiety by trying to make you look foolish or trying to provoke an argument.

While the aggressor is talking at you, breathe slowly and deeply. Repeat "Sticks and stones..." over and over in your mind. When you have to respond, give him one of the Concession Training "insult-comeback" lines. "Well, everyone's entitled to their own opinion" is a good one for openers. Should the discussion heat up, use one of the more potent insult-comeback lines: "Hey, man, don't you know when I'm kidding?" or "Come on, keep your shirt on." Commence laughing mildly, pat him gingerly on the shoulder, ask him how he's doing on his drink, say, "Hold on a minute, I don't want to miss a word of this!" Go pour yourself another drink, gulp it down, and slip quietly out the back door to your car. Continue "Sticks and Stones" all the way home.

If you were driven to the party by a friend, stand outside for five minutes, chanting, before you return to the party. If the aggressor approaches you again and starts the argument, back up, saying, "Where the hell have you been?" Then lean over and whisper in his ear, "Can you keep a secret?" As he nods, explain that you're sorry, but this "damned hepatitis has been giving me the runs." As he turns pale and begins to fall backward, take the drink out of his hand. Find your friend and leave.

4

The Pusillanimous Imperative

I admit the cowardice.
It is as universal as seasickness,
and matters just as little.

GEORGE BERNARD SHAW

Of all animal species, none is more cruel and rigid in its attitude toward cowardice than the human. For centuries Manic Concessives have lived beneath a yoke of shame for their inability to respond eye for eye, tooth for tooth in the face of conflict. They have been rebuked from infancy. They have been given role models of war heroes and martyred saints. They have been treated as second-class citizens. Unable to master even basic defense mechanisms, they are trapped in an anxiety-ridden limbo where they are too afraid to be assertive yet afraid to fully understand, accept, and respect the cowardice within them.

Few ever stop to realize that concession is a necessary, life-giving instinct in hundreds of animal species; that absolution and encouragement for their concession can be found throughout history, in the writings of great prophets and philosophers[9]; that, like the yin and yang of ancient Chinese thought, concession and aggression are but two sides of the same archetypal medallion, the former a prerequisite for the balance of nature and the continuation of orderly, civilized society.

ORACLE OF THE SPECIES

Ever since that first protozoan reared up its cilia and screamed to the second, "This tide pool ain't big enough for both of us!" the struggle for survival has been the primary concern of earthly life. Millions of years before man introduced such value judgments as "courage" and "cowardice," the central nervous systems of all animals, including man, were programmed to respond to conflict with either fight or flight reactions.[10]

---

[9]Immanuel Kant, for example, wrote *Ja, Ich Kant!* ("Yes, I Can't!"), a little-known essay in which he tried to explain to his followers why, if he was an enlightened German rationalist, he believed in going to church on Sunday "im fall das" (just in case).

[10]Turning pale when threatened, for example, is not cowardice. It's a purely involuntary biological defense: in case the person is slashed, the blood, having gone from the face surface, will not pour so profusely. And fainting is a biological defense against cardiac arrest.

Unlike modern-day machos who justify their own aggression and scorn cowards by using Darwin's survival-of-the-fittest doctrine out of context, Mother Nature saw cowardice (flight reaction) as not only a respectable but, above all, a necessary instinct for the survival of smaller animals, who were important in her overall plan but who could not be physically equipped to match the aggression of their predators. Had she projected onto these smaller animals a little-big-man complex, she would have condemned to early extinction hundreds of valuable species. Instead, she realized that the field mouse would stand little chance trying to duke it out with an owl, that the impala would soon be extinct should it feel compelled to stand there and take it when a leopard or lion attacked, that tiny reptiles would be little more than curious fossils had she programmed them to come out of hiding and exchange insults with hawks or eagles.

Thanks to the wisdom and compassion of Mother Nature, smaller, weaker animals have flourished right alongside their larger and more aggressive counterparts. Defense mechanisms— hiding, running, and adapting—have been the key to their survival and happiness. They can be the key to ours as well!

They Can Hide From It

The mole, a small, furry mammal, is on the menu of a number of forest predators. Because its tiny clawed hands were no match for the slashing talons of owls or the crushing jaws of snakes, it decided millenniums ago to sacrifice an adventurous land life filled with danger and trauma for a more stoic, but more secure, underground existence. Although it might occasionally daydream of being King of the Jungle, or imagine itself a rampaging mammoth bent on destruction, the mole is basically a realist, content to decrease its chances of everlasting blitz by living in a hole in the ground—a life dull and confining by rhinoceros standards, perhaps, but a life that affords all the food, shelter, and peace of mind it needs. Simply, the mole knows who he is, and who he isn't.

What can we learn from the humble mole? That one person's ceiling is another's floor. That freedom at the expense of your nerves is not freedom at all, but masochism. That there is a price tag on every life-style. That extremism in the pursuit of safety is no vice. That moderation in the pursuit of happiness is no virtue. That there are simply "different strokes for different folks."

Many other tiny creatures share the wisdom of the mole, some by employing a defense mechanism called protective coloration. Reptiles such as the chameleon, as well as many species of fish and fowl, escape predators by changing the color of their skin or feathers. By blending into their surroundings, by being paradigms of inconspicuousness, they remain unnoticed.

Some, when confronted by predators, can resort to more dramatic techniques. The squid, for example, escapes predators by first turning black and squirting a cloud of murky ink at its foe and then reversing its skin color to pink. While it scurries away, its predator swats around helplessly in the blackness. Other, deeper, sea creatures escape by squirting a luminous solution that temporarily blinds their predators.

The opossum, a small tree-dwelling mammal, is also a consummate actor. When it senses that a predator is near and that it is too far from the safety of a tree, it falls "dead" on the ground, simulating a heart attack ("playing 'possum"). The predator, torn for the moment between confusion and guilt, often hurries on, leaving the opossum to return to the security of its tree and the comfort of its family.

They Can Run Away From It

The gazelle is a sleek, graceful African deer that eats only fruits, roots, and wild berries. The lion and the leopard, by contrast, eat gazelles. So the gazelle has perfected keen senses to detect the advent of its enemies, and powerful speed and agility (more than 55 mph) to outrun and outmaneuver them. It can, if need be, leap more than twenty feet in a single bound, having developed this "cowardly" defense mechanism to an uncanny degree. To the gazelle it's not cowardice at all, it's simply Mother Nature's way. This animal was born free and won't be a slave to guilt.

The well-known ostrich is a master of concession. Centuries ago it lost its main defense mechanism—flight—by overeating. It became too heavy to escape into the air. Having no ability to change colors, it settled on developing long, strong legs for running. Sometimes, though, dense foliage prevents it from escaping on foot. When this happens, the ostrich sticks its head into the dirt or sand. Certainly it doesn't believe its 150-pound body becomes invisible! It simply prefers not to witness the sight of its own blood, should matters come to that. If the predator should pass by, however, the

ostrich returns to its nest or watering hole, relieved and thankful. It is not overcome by
shame for its concessive display. It doesn't get
depressed, or start drinking heavily, or start
taking its frustrations out on smaller ostriches.
The animal is happy to be alive and would do
it again should the need arise. To the ostrich
it's not cowardice, it's just common sense!

They Can Be Flexible About It

Many reptiles and amphibians evade their
predators by employing "breakaway" append-
ages. When caught, they detach themselves from
the limb or tail and hobble to safety. To com-
pensate for this rather severe defense mechanism, Mother Nature gives these creatures the
power to regenerate the lost portions of their
bodies. The lesson here is that giving up something to avoid giving up everything is not giving
up at all! Taking an insult to avoid the mental or
physical violence that an argument might produce is a very natural defense posture.

We too can learn to regenerate lost self-
esteem, if only we can learn to accept our limitations, to truly love ourselves for what we are, to
stop listening to the propaganda that insists we
are sick, we are second-class, we are sissies. We

are, as are all living things, children of Mother Nature, and our indelible birthright is survival.

COWARDICE OF THE GODS?

Who *were* these ancient visitors to our skies? Where did they come from? *Why* did they come? Why did they leave? Are they back? Why don't they just come down and level with us? What are they afraid of?

For years the mysteries of ancient astronauts have puzzled man. Were they some kind of extraterrestrial terrorists? Petty warlords from a Buck Rogers tale? Hardly. If they had been aggressors, they would have had a field day. Encountering no resistance from the technological dwarfs of Earth, they could have easily raped and pillaged the entire planet, sucked all the plutonium out of Utah, and set fire to the oceans.

Well, then, were they some kind of "cosmic druids" who came as giant black monoliths to enlighten man, to prepare his seed to travel beyond Jupiter, become an embryo at Consciousness II, and then spawn at his preordained fountain in the celestial godhead? Probably not. If they were mystics of that order, why have their descendants sunk to playing doctor on middle-aged couples from Vermont and slicing up cows in Arizona?

Given that the nearest solar system capable of supporting human life is Alpha Centauri, a whopping 25 trilliooo,ooo,ooo,ooon miles away; given that traveling five times the speed of our present-day spacecraft the journey would take over seventy years; given that no rational being in control of his courage would let himself get talked into sacrificing his adult life for a million-to-one-shot space expedition, you wonder. Were they neurotics? The butt of some infamous practical joke in another galaxy? Guinea pigs railroaded into getting soil samples for government scientists?

Five years ago I would have winced right along with you. But in the light of startling new evidence unearthed at sites around the world, there is an excellent chance that ancient visitors to our skies were, in fact, Cosmic Concessives—outcasts from highly evolved alien cultures who sympathized with the disorganization of psyche and warped priorities of early man. Encouraged to speak out by the immense amount of positive reinforcement—nay, *worship*—bestowed on them by the natives, they set about teaching our ancestors how to achieve an orderly, respectable civilization, a prerequisite for the survival of the Manic Concessive. Whether or not they succeeded is irrelevant. The fact is, they did the best they could.

These strange etchings on the Nasca Plain in Peru seem to take shape when viewed from a mile above the surface. Could the form in the center have been a landing site for the saucer-shaped craft of ancient astronauts? What do the hieroglyphics below it, translated as "Have a Nice Grycch," mean? Could it be a reassurance to fellow concessives that here was a safe, friendly place to land?

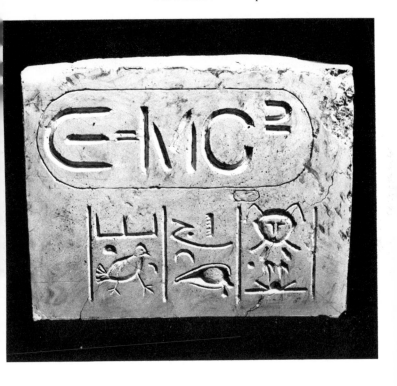

Found among ruins of the ancient city of Gizeh, this piece of rock was originally part of a large altar dedicated to the god-man Impotep. What appears to be an equation of some kind at top center corresponds to the hieroglyphics below, translated as "Evolution requires the acceptance of Manic Concessives (Squares)."

This wall painting, found among the remains of a primitive pub near Stonehenge, England, suggests that Cosmic Concessives (helmeted astronauts) were teaching our smaller, weaker ancestors to accept their limitations and ensure their survival by kneeling, pleading, and running when confronted by aggressive persons of greater size and strength.

Detouriata

Et harumd dereud facilis est er expedit distinct.
Nam liber tempor cumet conscient to factor turn
poem legum odioque civiuda. Et nobis eligent optio
conque nihil est impedit doming id quod maxim
religuard cupitat, quas nulla praid om umdant.

Improb pary minuit, los potius inflammad ut
coercend magist and et dodecendensse videantur.
Et invitat igitur vera raitio bene sanos as justitiam,
aequitated fidem. Neque loren ipsum dolor sit
amet, consectetur adipiscing elit, sed diam nonumy
ejusmod tempor incidunt ut labore et dolore magna
aliquam erat volupat.

Ut einim ad minim veniam, quis nostrud ceitation
ullam corpor suscipic laboris nisi ut alquip ex ea com-
mod consequet. Duis autem est vel eum irure dolor in
reprehenderit in voluptatae velit esse molestaie con-
sequat vel illum dolore eu fugiat nulla priatur.

At vero eos at accusam et justo odogio dignissum
qui blandit est praeent lupatum delenit aigue duos
dolor et molestias excepteur sin occeacat cupidatat
non provident, simil tempor sunt in culpa qui officia
de serunt mollit anim id est laborum et dolor fuga!

*One of the "Scrolls of Jupiter" (circa 310 B.C.), discovered in
Rome in 1691 by New England archaeologist Robert Melee.
Believed in Roman mythology to be "the word of our gods," the
scroll's message, as translated, is remarkably familiar.*

Detouriata

Slip quietly around the noise and haste, and remember what peace there may be in silence. As far as possible, surrender on good terms to all persons. Speak your mind quietly, and listen to others, for even the dull and ignorant might ask questions later.

Avoid loud and aggressive persons. They are more than vexations to the spirit. They could *kill* you! If you compare yourself to others you may be disappointed, for always there will be greater persons than you. Enjoy your imaginary achievements as well as your plans. Exercise caution in all your affairs; the world is already full of broken marriages.

But seriously. Be yourself. Gracefully surrender the things of youth, and anything else you can think of. Do not distress yourself with imagined fears. There are enough real causes for fear to worry about. Beyond a wholesome hedonism, be gentle with yourself. Play with yourself. After all, you are a child of the universe and you have a right to be here. And, whether you admit it or not, your cowardice is unfolding as it should.

Therefore be at peace with your God, whatever you need Him to be. And, in the noisy confusion of life, keep peace with your soul. With all its sham, drudgery, and broken dreams, the world isn't about to do it *for* you! Be careful. Watch out.

TOMORROW BELONGS TO US

We now know that we are special people; that we are Manic Concessives; that we are an oppressed minority whose time has come; that, in addition to inalienable rights, we have a sacred mission, a pusillanimous imperative, to do whatever is necessary to survive and to bring a permanent happiness to our lives.

Let's spend the next few days confirming our faith in the wisdom of Mother Nature. Let's vow to love, honor, and obey our natural instincts, in bad times and in worse. Let's try to find out if we can hire people to lobby and protest for us in Washington, D.C.

Let's forgive the aggressors who have wronged us in the past, and try to avoid them in the future. Let's forget the "pshrinks" who have given us dope instead of hope. Let's remember that concession is the better part of valium; that self-deprecating humor is the way to inner peace; that we can finally come out of the basement, move into the closet, and boldly whisper to the world, "I'm a Manic Concessive, and I'm proud!"

THE END

Appendix

Dynamics of Manic Concessive Behavior

FEAR OF PHYSICAL VIOLENCE

Many Manic Concessives go through life with a vague but pervasive paranoia which, particularly in the case of a male Manic Concessive, is rooted in childhood experiences with physical cowardice. It may have begun with a fistfight from which he walked or ran away— particularly traumatic if, in so doing, he betrayed a friend or displayed his weakness in full view of friends. In his mind the flight reaction was something involuntary and automatic. His heart began beating rapidly; he turned pale, developed a knot in the stomach, and lost contact with such abstracts as loyalty and valor. So afraid was he of getting hurt, he instinctively ran—unaware of the cause, or the ultimate cost, of his concessive display. He understood only afterward, when parents and peers scorched his ears with the burning labels "coward" or "sissy" or "scaredy-cat." The net result was often a profound devaluation in self-image, coupled with an immense guilt. Still, he could not understand the reason for his persecution. To him, his flight reaction had been a seizure for survival, an uncontrollable behavior which he knew, in his heart of hearts, that he would repeat again, should the occasion arise.

To the parents, however, it's always an embarrassing reflection on themselves. They scorn the child for something over which he has little or no control. This creates an impossible mental situation. To regain his parents' respect, he must either demonstrate courage the next time out or commence on a lifelong preoccupation with avoiding the possibility of there *being* a next time out. If he chooses the latter, he develops an ingratiating, aggressively friendly personality designed to help him avoid any sort of conflict that could lead to physical violence. This is the beginning of a lifetime of fear—and of covering up that fear, for fear of further self-devaluation.

At the first sign of courage impairment, many parents enroll their sons or daughters in self-defense classes. One patient who was enrolled in a karate class became quite proficient but confessed that, although he had won all his subsequent fights, he was nonetheless "scared to death" from start to finish. Another patient related that when he was forced to fight, he fought softly, trying to wrestle his opponent to the ground and then call for help. Even though he had the chance to finish off his foe, he was incapable of delivering any blood-producing blows. This was out of no sense of reverence for life, he assured me, but rather out of fear that, should he completely demolish his opponent, he would be the victim of a tenfold revenge.

For young Manic Concessives, fear of physical violence seems to always go hand in hand with a generalized fear of pain and danger: fear of the dentist, fear of getting a shot at the doctor's office, fear of doing the daring feats in which most children freely partake (hopping a train, jumping off a high dive, or speeding downhill on a bicycle). They do not delight, either, as do many children, in getting scared to death by horror movies, abandoned houses, or roller coasters.

As the Manic Concessive child approaches adulthood, this fear of physical violence becomes a more generalized paranoia, providing the "guiding darkness" for an anxiety-ridden, semireclusive existence. Adult Manic Concessives experience uptightness in any situation which could conceivably lead to physical harm. They tend to be jumpy when hearing people arguing loudly. They see conflict at every corner, muggers in every alley, rapists behind every bush. At night it's even worse. They walk with a brisk gait, even on a well-lit street, with arms swinging rigidly at their sides. This catatonic reaction is actually a physiological defense mechanism that, along with adrenaline flow, prepares them for flight. Most Manic Concessives also have an inordinate fear of dogs, and with good reason. Mean dogs, like aggressive people, can sense the fear. It excites them and compels them to attack. Thus, Manic Concessives get bitten more frequently than other people, which in turn makes them even more afraid of dogs, which in turn makes them walk faster and more rigidly in the presence of dogs, which, in turn, increases the likelihood of getting bitten again!

Manic Concessives feel uptight in bad sections of town, in unfamiliar liquor stores, in public restrooms, or at open parties or dances. Here again, fear of strangers and the violence they can produce is the behavior motivation. A male Manic Concessive might be hesitant about going on a fun-filled weekend camping trip in a beautiful mountain setting for fear of running into Hell's Angels or other wild animals. He may vote against going out for some great Chinese food (even though he has a craving), if his party wants to go to Chinatown to get it. He loses his appetite for sweet and sour pork thinking about getting involved in a Tong War, or being approached by some downtown transient, or, worst of all, running away should some young punks decide they like the looks of his girl friend. Most of his waking hours are spent, consciously or unconsciously, steering clear of potentially dangerous situations in which his cowardice will once again be dredged up in full view of friends and spectators alike.

Most Manic Concessives develop acute anxiety neurosis, which takes their paranoia a step further. They begin to feel fear in almost any situation. Just the thought of a dangerous situation can trigger the same response as the imminence of danger itself. Manic Concessives can get locked into depression for days worrying about hitting a pedestrian at some time in their lives, or getting hit themselves, or choking to death in a restaurant.

Understanding the deep-seated paranoia of Manic Concessives, it's easy to see how ineffective Assertiveness Training techniques can be in solving their problems. And with good reason! Assertiveness Training glosses over extreme fear of physical violence and concentrates instead on the more superficial symptoms and social inadequacies of unassertive behavior. Reversing a twenty- or thirty-year-old pattern of paranoia with behavior modification is tantamount to treating the criminally insane with graphology.[11]

Female Manic Concessives rarely suffer the trauma of physical cowardice in their youth. Because they are not expected to fight, and because young boys (even bullies) rarely subject them to hard-core physical violence, they are free to develop timid and retiring qualities without any attendant guilt and self-devaluation. In fact, young girls are often *rewarded* for being Manic Concessive ("sugar and spice and everything nice"). They are programmed to be docile and domestic, to find a good, strong man who will provide for them, and protect them from the harsh, cruel world.

Things are changing, though. Today, more and more women are shunning tradition, motherhood, and the male-dominated nuclear family structure, opting to find themselves in careers, hobbies, and outdoor activities. Female Manic Concessives are finding this particularly difficult, however, because their fear of physical

[11]Changing behavior patterns revealed through handwriting analysis by concentrating on changing the *handwriting* to resemble that of a well-adjusted individual.

violence is now coming home to them. With living in the cold world, far from the shelter of a canopy bed, comes living with traffic, alleys, strangers, and the soaring possibility of getting raped. Many have come to my office traumatized and disillusioned that the realities of their adult world don't conform to the social etiquette under which they prospered as children.

Just as I tell male Manic Concessives to find a nice girl to take care of them, I tell female Manic Concessives to find a nice man to take care of them.

FEAR OF MENTAL VIOLENCE

Interrelating with fear of physical violence is the fear of verbal or mental conflict which could lead to the disintegration of self-concept. To understand why Manic Concessives have a fragile self-image that is vulnerable to even the mildest form of mental cruelty, we must examine again the Manic Concessive's formative years.

In the childhood of most MCs we find either an excess of or a grave deficiency in the positive reinforcement (praise and support) received from parents and other authority figures. We've all seen the example of the neurotic extrovert whose poodle or other intelligent animal begins to take on the personality of the owner. The animal is a show-off: always dancing around, always needing attention, always anxious to be the center of activity. Upon receipt of any scolding, it pouts, gets depressed, or tries to punish the owner by not eating or by "do-doing" on the davenport. In the case of the poodle, we tend to think of this behavior as cute. It is far from cute, however, when we are talking of the young child.

Identity vacuum in Manic Concessives begins with a conscious or subconscious attempt by unassertive parents to discourage actions, feelings, and impulses that do not conform to their view of themselves. Because their children are a reflection of themselves to friends and family, they give praise and support when their children strictly adhere to their conception of social etiquette. They give positive reinforcement for the total suppression of the id (such natural, animalistic drives as sex, food, and aggression). Sex is rarely, if ever, discussed openly in these households. Children caught playing with themselves are punished without any reasonable explanation. The parents' uptightness about their own sexuality is transferred to the child.

While discouraging the id, these same parents

encourage the growth of the superego, society's code of behavioral etiquette. They reward the child for being sweet, nice, and polite and for always doing what they are told by authority figures ("goody-two-shoes syndrome"). Parents who are introverted neurotics do this not for the good of the child but rather to prevent embarrassment in front of their own friends and family. Parents who are extroverted neurotics (as in the case of the poodle owner) will encourage the child to dance around at family parties—to be a show-off—to constantly demonstrate some real or imagined precociousness. They receive vicariously the positive reinforcement showered on the child.

Couple these environmental conditions with a thirst for material comfort and security (common preoccupations of parents who grew up during the Great Depression), and you have a setting that discourages development of the child's ego (that unique concept of self which is independent of the id and superego and which makes decisions under minimal influence of either). The Manic Concessive child has been taught not to question, not to go against the norm, not to do anything that might cause embarrassment to its parents. This kind of sheltering prevents the child from learning how to

make real-life decisions and face the consequences. The constant reward for developing
the superego at the expense of the id and ego
discourages the formation of adjustive skills and
coping behaviors. Small wonder most Manic
Concessives have trouble dealing with the realities of life in the adult world, particularly conflict situations.

Children coming from such environments are
junkies for positive reinforcement. By the time
they begin to replace parental reinforcement
with peer reinforcement (teenage years), the pattern has been established. These young Manic
Concessives must look to others for the reassurance that they are doing what's "right" or
"good." Their sense of self-worth is not self-gen-
erating, because their conscience, or ego, was
never adequately developed. They become teth-
ered to the opinions of others. When praised,
they feel good about themselves. When others
dislike them, or offer even constructive criticism,
they feel devalued and become depressed.

This identity vacuum doesn't usually become
traumatic during the teenage years, because a
lack of ego is often fostered by peer groups,
clubs, and fraternities or sororities. Once life
begins to thin out one's acquaintances,
though—once career decisions and financial ob-

ligations become of prime importance—Manic Concessives find themselves seriously unprepared to cope. Because they possess few adjustive skills, life becomes one stress-producing conflict after another.

Like heroin addicts, Manic Concessives try to fill the void of identity, goals, and decisiveness with more and more positive reinforcement from others (a genuine search for identity at this late date seems too colossal a task). Ironically, though, the more positive reinforcement they receive, the more they need, and the more sensitive they become to negative reinforcement of any kind. A productive day, filled with achievement and encouragement from others, can be quickly shattered by even one negative innuendo. They have no identity, no central core of reference to which they can retreat under stress. They are preoccupied not with "who I am" but with "who I *should* be." They think not of "what I want to do with my life" but rather, "what I *should* be doing with my life." They always see themselves in the context of others, always looking at friends and lovers as parents, rather than as equals.

This is what I mean by fear of mental violence. Having no genuine identity, Manic Concessives are always at the mercy of others. They must work overtime to avoid the possibility of conflict. Negative reinforcement damages whatever self-esteem they have, so they must always try to be ingratiating, always try to do the right thing, always try to make people like and accept them.

From this neurotic need for positive reinforcement comes also a fear of emotion. Because of childhood conditioning, Manic Concessives constantly search for emotional responses that are "appropriate" rather than "felt." Because the expression of emotions was suppressed in childhood, Manic Concessives suffer from chronic insincerity. Fearing conflict, they are often overly friendly, extending lavish greetings to people they privately can't stand, feigning rapt attention listening to people who "bore my ass off," exploding with excitement about ideas they couldn't really "care less about." Insincerity can be particularly poignant at Christmastime. Manic Concessives have no trouble giving gifts but feel uneasy being on the receiving end of a gift, worrying about how the response "should sound" (what if they don't like the gift?), worrying about being able to muster up a sincere thank-you, complete with eye contact. In any situation that demands a simple, heartfelt response, a Manic Concessive feels awkward.

MCs can also be extremely circumlocutious, especially when trying to make a direct request. They wade slowly into the question, sensing and processing each "mini-reaction" as their words get closer and closer to clarifying the request. Because of their acute fear of rejection, and their guilt about anyone sacrificing anything to do something for them (don't want to be a burden), they carefully phrase their words until the very end, always leaving themselves the option of retreat. If their listener politely begins to turn down the request they jump in, cutting him off in mid-sentence with something like "Hey, no problem," "Maybe next week," or "Hey, don't worry about it."

Fearing controversy, Manic Concessives avoid taking a stand. They seldom voice an opinion, because they seldom have one. For fear of alienating one side or the other in a dispute, they point out the good on both sides. They always see things as too complex to judge hastily, too close to call, or too touchy to touch. They are deathly afraid of getting into any situation which could lead to conflict or rejection.

At a certain point in adult life, Manic Concessives become painfully aware of the constant charade, the constant cover-up, the constant other-directed quality of their lives. Their pervasive fear of mental and physical violence brings on more severe symptoms of anxiety neurosis. They become chronic apprehensives, feeling a dull dread no matter how well things seem to be going. They not only have difficulty making decisions, but once made, they worry excessively about possible errors or dangerous consequences. As soon as one cause for anxiety is swept away, they find another to take its place.

Even after going to bed, Manic Concessives cannot find relief. They review each mistake in the day, real or imagined. They spend time reviewing past failures, and the remaining time with failures looming in the future. If they do manage to fall asleep (MCs are notorious insomniacs), their dream life takes over from there. Their cerebral circuitry is so complex, these dreams are never simple parables. They often have a cast of thousands—menacing people from the past, menacing people not yet encountered, old lovers, dead friends, and bad checks. People turn into animals, into other people, and back again. MCs frequently dream of being choked, of falling off high places, or of being chased by murderers and not being able to escape because their legs will move only in slow motion. When they scream for help, nothing comes out. They wake up seconds before their "death," traumatized and, upon reflection, disgusted that they don't have the courage to kill themselves.